THE FOREST
GAME GUIDE

Your Ultimate Companion to Discover

Secret Techniques, Conquer Every Brutal

Challenge and Leave your Mark on the

Unforgiving Wilderness with Expert Tricks

and Strategies

George Hannon

Table Of Contents:

Introduction

*T*he Forest, an immersive and challenging survival game developed by Endnight Games, thrusts players into a mysterious and perilous world. Set on a remote, seemingly deserted island, the game combines elements of survival, exploration, and horror, providing a unique and engaging gaming experience. As players navigate through dense forests, mysterious caves, and encounter hostile mutants, they must master the art of survival against all odds.

Overview of The Forest

The Forest begins with a harrowing plane crash, leaving the player stranded in a lush and dangerous environment. The island is not as uninhabited as it first appears; mutants and other mysterious creatures roam freely, creating an ever-present threat. The dynamic day-night cycle and realistic weather conditions add to the immersive atmosphere, requiring players to adapt and strategize for different challenges.

One of the distinctive features of The Forest is its focus on realism in survival mechanics. Players must manage hunger, thirst, and stamina while also dealing with the psychological impact of their surroundings. The environment is fully destructible, allowing players to chop down trees for resources and build intricate structures for shelter and defense.

The game also incorporates a storyline, subtly revealed through scattered clues and environmental storytelling. As players explore the island, they uncover the dark secrets behind the mutants and their connection to the player's character. This narrative depth adds an extra layer of intrigue to the overall gaming experience.

Purpose of the Guide

The purpose of this guide is to serve as a comprehensive companion for both new and experienced players of The Forest. Navigating the complexities of the game can be daunting, especially for those venturing into the survival genre for the first time. For seasoned players, this guide aims to provide advanced strategies and insights to enhance their gameplay.

Whether you're struggling to survive the initial moments after the crash or seeking to build an impenetrable fortress against the island's dangers, this guide offers valuable tips, strategies, and in-depth explanations. From crafting essential tools to choosing the optimal base location, each section is designed to empower players with the knowledge needed to thrive in The Forest's unforgiving environment.

Beyond survival basics, the guide delves into advanced crafting, exploration techniques, and multiplayer strategies. It covers the nuances of base building, providing a roadmap for creating secure shelters and fortresses. The narrative aspect of the game is also explored, offering guidance on uncovering the island's mysteries.

By presenting a well-structured and detailed guide, the aim is to demystify the intricacies of The Forest, fostering a more enjoyable and rewarding gaming experience. Whether players seek a story-driven adventure, cooperative multiplayer challenges, or simply wish to survive the island's perils, this guide aims to be a valuable resource, aiding players in their quest for mastery in The Forest's dynamic and unpredictable world.

Chapter 1

Getting Started

Embarking on The Forest's Harrowing Journey

Step into the unforgiving embrace of The Forest's wilderness as the plane wreckage becomes your unlikely starting point. Amidst the chaos, you awaken alone, disoriented, and fueled by the distant cries of your son, Timmy, echoing through the thick foliage. The decisions you make now will shape your survival amidst the island's challenges.

Surviving the Crash and Scavenging

Escape the twisted metal of the plane, driven by adrenaline, and survey the scattered remnants of your former life. Amidst the debris, you'll find crucial supplies— a **flare gun**, a **lighter**, and a **first-aid kit**—essential for your early survival. Don't overlook the **axe** lodged in the cockpit door, your initial tool for both crafting and defense.

Gathering Vital Resources

Step beyond the wreckage into the oppressive wilderness filled with unseen creatures. The humid air resonates with chirps, a constant reminder of your shared space with the unknown. Your focus now shifts to securing basic necessities:

- **Food and Water:**
Harvest berries and mushrooms cautiously near the crash site and locate a freshwater source, ensuring to boil it for safety.

- **Shelter:**
Construct or find a refuge from the harsh elements and nightly predators, be it a natural cave or a rudimentary lean-to.

- **Clothing:**
Seek dry clothes within wreckage or from fallen logs, as wet garments drain stamina, leaving you vulnerable.

- **Crafting Materials:**

Gather sticks, stones, and leaves—these form the foundation of your survival tools, from weapons to firestarters.

Choosing Your Path

With immediate needs met, the vast and perilous island awaits exploration. Consider these options:

- **Following Timmy's Cries:**
Your primary goal, but beware of potential traps and ambushes set by the island's cannibalistic inhabitants.

- **Exploring the Crash Site:**

Uncover valuable supplies and clues about your journey by examining documents, luggage, and hidden compartments.

- **Heading Towards the Beach:**

Access to fish and shellfish for sustenance, but be cautious of aggressive sharks patrolling the waters.

- **Climbing a Hill:**

Gain altitude for a better view, identifying landmarks and potential threats.

Additional Considerations:

- **North:**

Journey towards the snowy peak of Mount Kananaskis for breathtaking views, encountering mutated creatures adapted to the cold, and discovering rare resources.

- **West:**

Traverse the coastline with sandy beaches, hidden caves, and opportunities for fishing and scavenging, but beware of lurking dangers.

- **East:**

Explore lush valleys and dense forests teeming with wildlife and resources, but stay vigilant for hidden dangers like sinkholes and traps.

- **South:**

Venture towards mysterious sinkholes and ancient ruins guarded by powerful mutants and cannibalistic tribes, a challenging but potentially rewarding route.

Remember, every decision carries risks in The Forest's watchful environment.

Bonus Tips:

- Attend to your mental health; build fires for warmth and comfort and create makeshift effigies of Timmy.
- Monitor the sun's position for navigation.
- Pay attention to the sounds of the forest to identify potential threats.
- Embrace experimentation; The Forest rewards curiosity. Try different crafting combinations and uncover hidden secrets.

The first hours in The Forest shape your entire adventure. By following these tips and making informed decisions, you'll navigate the wilderness and unveil the mysteries that lie within. The forest is a demanding teacher, yet it offers vast rewards for the brave. So, grasp your axe, take a deep breath, and step into the unknown. The Forest awaits. Stay tuned for the next part, where we explore the art of crafting—essential for survival against the island's myriad threats.

Chapter 2

Survival Basics

Amidst the rustling leaves, the damp soil beneath your feet, and the distant echoes of hidden creatures, you find yourself embraced by the unforgiving realm of The Forest. Here, survival rests upon the triumvirate of crafting essential tools, securing sustenance, and erecting havens against the capricious elements and lurking dangers. Let's navigate through these primal necessities, arming you with the knowledge to endure the challenges that lie ahead.

Crafting Tools and Weapons

While bare hands may grant you a transient existence, true survival demands the crafting of tools. Initiate your journey with a modest stone axe, chiseled from the island's rocky veins. This primitive implement opens up a plethora of possibilities – from felling trees for logs, collecting sticks and leaves, to mining rocks for flint, and even fending off small adversaries.

As you delve deeper into the wild, your crafting repertoire burgeons like a blossoming vine. Master the art of weaving sticks and leaves into makeshift spearpoints, creating weapons for ranged hunting and thrusting attacks. Produce bone daggers for stealthy takedowns and transform clubs into brutal warhammers for devastating blows. Advanced crafting stations, such as drying racks and fires, empower you to preserve food, concoct potent healing elixirs, and fashion bows and arrows for precision hunting.

Yet, tools transcend mere instruments of conquest. Implement basic traps to capture rabbits and birds, construct cages to domesticate these surprisingly palatable avian companions. Fashion fishing rods from sticks and rope, casting lines into serene ponds and rivers to secure a fresh catch. Remember, adaptability is paramount – a makeshift torch from leaves and sap illuminates your path, and a robust log raft broadens your hunting grounds and potential discoveries.

Hunting and Gathering Food

The island offers sustenance for those who discern where to seek. Begin by foraging mushrooms and berries, mastering the art of distinguishing between the nourishing and the perilous. Spearhead rabbits and birds for immediate rewards, employ well-placed arrows for larger prey like deer, and appreciate the humble fish for a constant source of freshwater provisions.

While hunting yields instant gratification, a sustainable food source should not be overlooked. Cultivate berry bushes and herb gardens near your refuge, transforming them into a self-replenishing pantry. Master the art of trapping small animals like lizards and turtles, ensuring a reliable protein source without the thrill of the chase. Remember, variety is the cornerstone – a diverse diet sustains your health and elevates your spirits.

Yet, food transcends mere sustenance. The act of hunting, gathering, and tending your garden weaves you into the island's rhythm, intertwining you with its intricate tapestry. Each triumphant kill, each thriving plant, murmurs a silent victory, a testament to your resilience and resourcefulness.

Building Shelter

As night descends, shrouding the forest in obsidian darkness, the primordial need for shelter takes precedence. Your initial refuge may be a rudimentary lean-to nestled against a colossal tree trunk, but you are not merely seeking transient respite. You are a builder, a creator, and The Forest eagerly anticipates the imprint of your ingenuity.

Amass logs and sticks, molding them into walls and roofs. Master the craft of fashioning rope from yucca fibers, binding your creation into a robust dwelling. Integrate a firepit for warmth and light, a drying rack to preserve your precious food, and storage shelves to organize your burgeoning collection of tools and trinkets. Venture into advanced structures like treehouses and underwater caves, pushing the boundaries of your architectural prowess.

Shelter surpasses mere physical protection; it is a canvas for your identity, a testament to your skills and determination. Embellish your walls with animal trophies and gathered relics, construct inviting sleeping quarters and efficient crafting stations. As your sanctuary expands, it transforms into a beacon of hope, a symbol of your conquest over the wilderness.

Remember, these are merely the initial strokes on the survival canvas. The Forest beckons as a playground of possibilities, urging you to experiment, refine, and adapt. Craft not only tools but strategies. Hunt not just prey but knowledge. Build not merely shelters but a narrative of resilience in the face of the unknown.

Step into The Forest's verdant embrace, armed with these basics and a fiery resolve. Carve your path, find your rhythm, and inscribe your unique chapter in the island's ever-evolving saga.

Chapter 3

Exploration

*I*n the heart of The Forest lies an untamed wilderness, a vast expanse that intertwines beauty and peril. Nature's secrets, valuable resources, and elusive answers are concealed within its dense foliage, but to navigate this uncharted territory requires a keen sense of direction and a profound respect for the indigenous cannibals and mutants. This section aims to illuminate the art of exploration, arming you with the knowledge to traverse the landscape, pinpoint vital locations, and emerge triumphant from encounters with hostile inhabitants.

Navigating the Map

- **Varied Terrain and Distinct Landmarks:**

The Forest boasts a spectrum of biomes, ranging from luxuriant forests and rugged cliffs to sunlit beaches and ominous caves. Mastery of recognizing landmarks such as mountains, rivers, and unique rock formations is paramount for orientation and retracing your steps to familiar ground.

- **GPS Navigation and Marking:**

Your dependable GPS device serves as the primary tool for navigation, revealing points of interest, cave entrances, and your ongoing objectives. Intelligently deploy markers to highlight discovered resources, potential base sites, or perilous zones.

- **Crafted Maps:**

Seasoned explorers can fashion physical maps using cloth and charcoal, providing a tangible depiction of explored regions. This proves invaluable for planning extensive journeys or sharing newfound knowledge in multiplayer ventures.

- **Celestial Guidance:**

Observe the sun's movement for directional cues, especially when landmarks are absent.

During nocturnal hours, constellations offer a celestial guide akin to the sun.

Key Locations and Points of Interest

- **Mysterious Caves:**

Beneath the surface, intricate labyrinths house valuable resources, markers of lore, and occasionally concealed bunkers. Exercise caution against cave-ins, traps, and the presence of lurking mutants.

- **Enigmatic Sinkholes:**

These abyssal pits serve as portals to the island's underworld, unveiling mutant lairs, peculiar anomalies, and potential new avenues to explore.

- **Primitive Cannibal Camps:**

Crude settlements provide loot and insights into the island's inhabitants, but expect confrontations with hostile forces.

- **Scattered Aircraft Wreckage:**

The remnants of your plane are poignant reminders of your arrival, harboring essential survival items and equipment.

- **Covert Military Bunkers:**

Concealed installations house potent weapons, crafting materials, and valuable insights into the island's history. Discovery demands acute observation and puzzle-solving skills.

Dealing with Enemies

- **Stealth Mastery:**

Outsmart cannibals and mutants with ease. Utilize a crouched stance, seek cover in foliage, and exploit natural sound barriers like waterfalls to remain undetected.

- **Strategic Engagement:**

Avoid unnecessary combat. Assess situations, draw enemies away from each other, and prioritize evading larger groups or formidable mutants.

- **Tactical Traps and Environmental Perils:**

Lay snares, strategically position explosives, and lead enemies into environmental hazards such as fire pits or sinkholes for strategic advantage.

- **Combat Proficiency:**

Understand the strengths and weaknesses of various weapons. Hone skills in dodging, parrying, and aiming for headshots to maximize combat effectiveness.

- **Fire Dynamics:**

Employ fire for illumination, cooking, and enemy deterrence, but exercise caution in the arid environment to prevent unintentional blazes.

In the realm of exploration, patience and adaptability reign supreme. Learn from mistakes, embrace experimentation, and fear not the uncharted. The Forest favors the inquisitive and the courageous. Armed with knowledge and caution, unravel the island's enigmas and emerge victorious from its depths.

Chapter 4

Advanced Crafting

Surviving in The Forest transcends basic needs; it's a venture into innovation, where crafting goes beyond mere tools and shelters. It's a realm where creativity transforms metal scraps into instruments of power, and the elements themselves become weapons against lurking threats.

Harnessing Circuit Boards: Unlocking Technological Marvels

In hidden bunkers and caves, discover the rare treasure of circuit boards, unleashing a new era of crafting:

- **Flare Gun:**

Combine a circuit board, lighter, duct tape, and alcohol for a fiery retribution against cannibals, creating a potent tool for defense and area denial.

- **Remote Detonator:**

Fuse a circuit board with a watch, duct tape, and a battery to turn strategically placed Molotovs into remotely triggered explosions, catching enemies off guard.

- **Advanced Crafting Table:**

Merge a circuit board with a basic crafting table and duct tape to access unprecedented items, from advanced tools and traps to high-tech weaponry.

Crafting Explosives

In this unforgiving landscape, diplomacy may fail, but a well-placed explosion can convey a powerful message:

- **Molotov Cocktails:**
Combine rag and alcohol for a quick and fiery weapon; add tree sap for an extra punch.

- **Sticky Bombs:**
Craft adhesive grenades by combining a Molotov with duct tape and coins, ensuring explosions cling to enemies.

- **Dynamite:**

Answering with brute force, create dynamite by combining a circuit board with alcohol, coins, and a watch, capable of leveling entire cannibal villages.

Upgrading Weapons and Tools

Upgrade your basic tools into instruments of mastery, turning the hostile world into your dominion:

- **Upgraded Axe:**

Enhance your basic axe with duct tape, rope, and bones for a more durable and damaging tool, capable of felling trees, defeating enemies, and harvesting resources efficiently.

- **Bone Armor:**

Craft protection from cannibals and mutants by combining bones, cloth, and duct tape into gruesome yet effective armor.

- **Crossbow:**

Transform your basic bow into a silent hunter with deadly accuracy and power by adding a circuit board, rope, and feathers.

Advanced Crafting:

Explore the vast potential of advanced crafting by experimenting with different combinations and uncovering rare components in hidden bunkers:

- **Animal Traps:**

Capture valuable animals for food and resources using shock traps for mutants or sonic traps for explosive cannibal ambushes.

- **Mutated Weaponry:**

Craft unique weapons from mutated creatures, like a bone bow from a Bone Armor mutant or a weapon forged from a Shark's teeth.

- **Tech-Powered Armor:**

With circuit boards and experimentation, envision wearing technological wonders, such as a helmet granting night vision or armor deflecting attacks with an electric surge.

The world of advanced crafting in The Forest is a playground for inventive minds. So, seize your tools, gather materials, and unleash your inner engineer. The forest awaits, revealing its secrets only to those daring to push the boundaries of what's possible.

Chapter 5

Mastering Base Construction: Fortifying Your Refuge in The Forest

Surviving the brutal landscape of The Forest hinges on transforming your base from a mere shelter into an impervious stronghold against cannibalistic horrors. Craft a secure and efficient haven with foresight, resourcefulness, and strategic cunning. Let's delve into pivotal strategies to elevate your base from a vulnerable shack to an impenetrable bastion.

Choosing an Ideal Location

In The Forest, your base's location is paramount. A poorly chosen spot exposes you to enemy incursions, resource scarcity, and inconvenient travel. Consider these critical factors:

- **Natural Defenses:**
Leverage the terrain! Construct against cliffs or rock walls for instant fortification on one side. Explore caves or elevated plateaus for natural chokepoints against enemies.

- **Resource Richness:**
Proximity to vital resources like water, food, and building materials reduces scavenging time. Choose sites near freshwater, fertile forests, and cave entrances abundant in flint and clay.

- **Strategic Distance:**

Balance isolation with practicality. Find a sweet spot between safety from cannibal camps and convenient access to key locations like the plane crash site or story-driven points of interest.

- **Enemy Patrols:**

Observe enemy patrol patterns. Avoid building directly in their path, yet maintain proximity to potential allies like friendly tribes.

Building Formidable Defenses

Once your strategic plot is secured, erect walls and set traps. Defense involves layering obstacles and delaying enemies, not creating an impenetrable fortress. Consider these effective strategies:

- **Multi-layered Walls:**

Upgrade from stick walls to materials like logs and stone. Create double-walled sections with inner and outer layers. Integrate defensive spikes and burning effigies to deter attackers.

- **Moat Master:**

Dig trenches to funnel enemies and slow their advance. Use bridges or ziplines for personal access while obstructing enemies. Water acts as a natural barrier; incorporate nearby lakes or streams into your defense.

- **Trappy Territory:**

Deploy traps strategically near chokepoints and entrances. Use snares, tripwires, remote explosives, and decoy dummies to hinder and divert enemies.

- **Turrets and Towers:**

Build elevated platforms and towers for a tactical advantage. Mount crossbow turrets and flare guns for long-range defense. Fortify elevated positions with ladders or rope ramps.

Effective Wall and Trap Placement

Strategic placement maximizes defense effectiveness. Consider these specific tips:

- **Chokepoint Control:**

Place walls and traps in narrow passages to concentrate enemies, making them easier to deal with.

- **Layered Deterrence:**

Distribute traps at varying distances for layered defense, forcing enemies to expend resources before reaching your inner sanctum.

- **Decoy Ambushes:**

Lure enemies into traps by placing enticing items strategically.

- **Strategic Flanking:**

Include hidden entrances or escape routes to flank and ambush distracted enemies.

Adaptability is Crucial:

Base building is an ongoing process. Adapt and redesign defenses as you encounter new threats. Experiment with walls, traps, and terrain manipulation to create a base matching your playstyle.

This exploration of base building strategies forms a strong foundation for conquering the wilderness. Keep your wits sharp, axe ready, and defenses unbreachable. May your base stand as a testament to your resilience and ingenuity in the face of The Forest's cannibalistic darkness!

Chapter 6

Long-Term Survival

Embarking on the journey in The Forest initiates a trial of wit and resilience. Yet, true expertise lies in establishing a sustainable existence, where the forest transforms into both provider and fortress. This guide delves into the intricacies of long-term survival, offering insights not only for enduring the wilderness but thriving within its unforgiving grasp.

Sustainable Food Sources

1. Beyond the Hunt:

While hunting proves effective, exclusive reliance leads to depletion and danger. Embrace sustainable methods such as:

- **Farming Dynamics:** Cultivating vegetables, fruits, and herbs ensures a continuous supply. Optimize your farm layout, experimenting with various crops for maximum yield.

- **Strategic Trapping:** Employ snares and cages to capture smaller creatures, like rabbits and birds. These low-maintenance traps offer a consistent source of protein when placed in high-animal-activity zones.

- **Art of Fishing:** Master fishing techniques and enhance your rods to access diverse fish species. Establish fishing huts strategically for a convenient supply of food and water.

2. Animal Harmony:

Taming deer, rabbits, and boars transforms your surroundings into a living pantry. Breeding animals guarantees a steady food supply and provides crafting materials, such as leather.

3. Harvesting Bounty:

Edible plants and mushrooms supplement your diet. Learn to identify nutritious options, rotating gathering locations to prevent depletion.

Advanced Crafting and Upgrades

- **Tech Tree Prowess:**

Unlocking advanced blueprints introduces new tools, weapons, and structures. Prioritize crafting enhancements aligned with your playstyle, whether fortifying your base, refining combat skills, or perfecting farming techniques.

- **Specialized Instruments:**

Craft advanced tools like bone armor, scuba gear, and explosives. These open new exploration, combat, and resource-gathering avenues.

- **Elevated Bases:**

Upgrade beyond basic shelters. Incorporate defensive structures like traps, walls, and mounted turrets. Add structures like greenhouses, workshops, and animal pens for enhanced self-sufficiency.

- **Navigational Innovations:**

Craft rafts and boats for efficient water travel. Ziplines offer a thrilling way to navigate between elevated points in your base.

Preparing for Late-Game Challenges

- **Mutant Confrontation:**

Craft potent weapons—molotov cocktails, bombs, and upgraded spears—to combat late-game mutant challenges.

- **Fortifying Your Haven:**

Late-game mutants pose threats. Strategically plan defenses with traps, turrets, and strategically placed fire to deter and eliminate attackers.

- **Unraveling Sinkhole Secrets:**

Dive into mysterious depths, armed with upgraded scuba gear and potent underwater weapons, to unveil valuable resources and lore.

- **The Ultimate Showdown:**

Equip yourself with top-tier gear, fortify your base, and strategize before facing the climactic challenge.

Tips for Prolonged Survival:

- **Diversification Wisdom:**

Avoid relying on a single food source or strategy. Adapt to the evolving environment, utilizing all available resources.

- **Proactive Planning:**

Don't wait for resources to deplete. Plan ahead, gather materials, and prepare for future needs.

- **Exploration and Experimentation:**

Venture beyond your comfort zone, exploring new areas for hidden benefits and secrets.

- **Embrace Challenges:**

The Forest thrives on difficulty. Embrace challenges, learn from setbacks, and progress towards mastery.

By mastering these long-term survival strategies, you evolve from a mere survivor into a forest master. Build a flourishing haven, conquer challenges, and uncover the secrets within The Forest's heart. Long-term survival demands not just endurance but adaptation, innovation, and an unwavering spirit of exploration. Sharpen your axe, refine your skills, and embrace the wild. The forest awaits, rewarding those who respect its unforgiving beauty.

Chapter 7

Mastering Multiplayer

$\mathcal{E}$mbarking on the cannibal-infested peninsula of The Forest takes on a whole new dimension when experienced in its exhilarating cooperative mode. While tackling the wild alone presents its own challenges, navigating the dynamics of multiplayer demands a unique skill set. Here's a comprehensive guide to not just surviving but thriving in The Forest alongside your fellow survivors:

Cooperative Strategies

- **Strategic Division:**

Teamwork is essential, but efficiency lies in dividing tasks. Assign roles based on individual strengths. One player can focus on construction and resource gathering, while another explores caves and hunts for sustenance. Rotate tasks to keep everyone engaged.

- **Knowledge is Strength:**

Communication is paramount. Share discoveries, mark crucial locations on the map, and freely exchange resources. Stay informed about potential dangers and coordinate tactics when facing adversaries.

- **Establish a Shared Haven:**

Construct a central base that acts as a home away from home. Allocate areas for crafting, sleeping, and storage, ensuring everyone has a secure retreat. Consider building outposts near resource-rich zones to facilitate exploration.

- **Combat Harmony:**

Facing cannibals or mutants requires teamwork. Strategically combine attacks, using ranged weapons to weaken foes before melee fighters deliver the finishing blow. Revive fallen comrades promptly and share healing items.

- **Sharing is Caring:**

Avoid hoarding resources. Freely share food, water, and crafting materials to ensure everyone remains healthy and well-equipped. Remember, your friends' survival is intertwined with yours.

Dealing with Other Players

- **Allies or Adversaries?:**

Online players may not share your intentions. Be cautious of strangers and set server rules or passwords to play with trusted friends.

- **Guard Against Griefing:**

Griefing can disrupt multiplayer experiences. Monitor shared resources and structures. Address intentional disruptions calmly or vote to remove disruptive players.

- **Communication is Key (Revisited):**

Clear communication is crucial when conflicts arise. Discuss boundaries and expectations before starting the game. Resolve accidental issues through calm conversation and a willingness to compromise.

- **Embrace the Unpredictable:**

Multiplayer thrives on unpredictability. Be prepared for mishaps, friendly fire, and moments of unexpected teamwork. Embrace the chaos and relish the unique experiences that arise from playing with others.

- **Remember the Common Goal:**

Whether finding Timmy, uncovering the island's secrets, or surviving the forest, prioritize cooperation, communication, and mutual respect.

Bonus Tips:

- **Roleplay Dynamics:**

Assign unique roles, like a dedicated hunter, trapmaster, or lorekeeper, to add fun and immersion to your shared experience.

- **Unleash the Absurd:**

Have fun! Build unconventional structures, stage pranks, or organize impromptu mutant gladiator matches. The forest is your playground.

- **Document Your Odyssey:**

Capture screenshots, record funny moments, and share stories to create lasting memories of your adventures.

Remember, The Forest's multiplayer mode offers a unique chance to share the thrill of survival. By following these tips, create a collaborative experience where teamwork, trust, and humor pave the way for conquering the island's dangers and forging lasting memories. So, rally your friends, wield your axes, and face the forest together!

Chapter 8

Troubleshooting and Tips

As players venture into the mysterious and perilous world of The Forest, encountering challenges is inevitable. From technical hiccups to navigating the intricacies of survival, this section aims to provide a comprehensive guide to troubleshooting common issues and offering additional tips for a successful playthrough. Let's dive into the intricacies of addressing challenges and enhancing your overall gaming experience.

Common Issues and Solutions

1. Performance Concerns:

- **Issue:** Players might experience performance issues, including lag or frame rate drops.

- **Solution:** Adjust graphics settings in the game to find a balance between visual quality and performance. Lowering certain settings like shadows and textures can significantly improve frame rates.

2. Crashes and Freezes:

- **Issue:** The game may crash or freeze unexpectedly.

- **Solution:** Make sure your graphics drivers are current. Additionally, verify the integrity of the game files through the Steam client. If issues persist, consider adjusting in-game settings or running the game in compatibility mode.

3. Multiplayer Connection Problems:

- **Issue:** Difficulties in connecting to multiplayer servers or experiencing frequent disconnections.

- **Solution:** Check your internet connection stability. If the problem persists, try joining servers with lower ping. It's also advisable to close unnecessary background applications to optimize network performance.

4. Save Game Corruption:

- **Issue:** Save files may become corrupted, leading to progress loss.

- **Solution:** Regularly back up your save files manually. In case of corruption, having a recent backup ensures minimal progress loss. Additionally, consider turning on Steam Cloud synchronization for an extra layer of save file protection.

5. Audio Glitches:

- **Issue:** Audio may cut out or become distorted during gameplay.

- **Solution:** Update your audio drivers and check in-game audio settings. If issues persist, lowering audio quality settings might resolve glitches. Some players have reported success by changing the audio output device.

6. Control and Input Problems:

- **Issue:** Unresponsive controls or input lag.

- **Solution:** Ensure your input devices are functioning correctly. Calibrate controllers if necessary. If using mods or third-party software, verify compatibility and update as needed.

Switching to a different input device can also help troubleshoot control issues.

7. Graphics Glitches:

- **Issue:** Visual anomalies such as flickering textures or graphical artifacts.

- **Solution:** Update graphics drivers and experiment with different graphics settings. Turning off certain visual effects might resolve glitches. If using mods, check for compatibility issues with the game version.

8. Inventory Conundrums:

- **Issue:** Items vanishing from your inventory?

- **Solution:** Try crafting, dropping, or restarting. If all else fails, cautiously deploy a console command like "inv_give #itemid" (replace # with item ID).

9. Cannibal Quirks:

- **Issue:** Cannibals acting odd?
- **Solution:** If they get stuck or teleport, give them a nudge or reload the area for a quick fix.

10. Missing Timmy Markers:

- **Issue:** If Timmy's markers vanish
- **Solution:** Explore caves and underwater spots. He might be hiding where you least expect.

Additional Tips for a Successful Playthrough

1. Environmental Awareness:

Always be aware of your surroundings. The island is dynamic, and threats can come from unexpected directions. Pay attention to environmental cues, like changes in weather or unusual sounds, which can signal impending danger.

2. Resource Conservation:

Manage resources wisely. While it may be tempting to gather everything in sight, consider the weight of each item and its immediate usefulness. Prioritize essential items and avoid overburdening yourself, especially during exploration.

3. Nighttime Preparations:

Night brings increased dangers. Prepare for nighttime encounters by having a light source, weapons, and a secure shelter. Consider planning daytime activities strategically to minimize exposure during the night.

4. Cooperative Play Strategies:

If playing in multiplayer mode, communication and coordination are key. Establish roles within the group, share resources, and coordinate base building efforts. Working together enhances survival chances against the island's challenges.

5. Exploration in Groups:

Exploring the island is safer in groups. Traveling with companions provides additional firepower and support during encounters with mutants. Coordinate exploration routes and share discoveries for a more efficient playthrough.

6. Regular Saving:

Save progress regularly. The Forest does not have an auto-save feature, so manually saving your game ensures that you won't lose significant progress in case of unexpected events or challenges.

7. Experiment with Crafting:

Feel free to explore and try different crafting approaches. Combine different resources to discover new recipes and improve your survival toolkit. Crafting more advanced items opens up new possibilities for defense and exploration.

8. Stay Informed About Updates:

The game may receive updates and patches. Stay informed about the latest developments by checking official channels or community forums. Updates might introduce new features, address bugs, or enhance gameplay mechanics.

9. Stealth Mastery:

Cannibals are easily alarmed. Crouch, use foliage as cover, and opt for ranged weapons to avoid direct conflicts.

Extra Survival Strategies:

- **Trainable Mutants:** Patiently "tame" certain mutants for temporary allies against enemies.
- **Kiting Tactics:** Lure cannibals away by running and maintaining distance.
- **Flare Gun Tactics:** Use flares to attract enemies or burn down villages for distraction.
- **Waterfront Building:** Challenging but rewarding, build platforms on water for safety and new resources.

In conclusion, troubleshooting common issues and incorporating additional tips into your gameplay can significantly enhance your experience in The Forest. From addressing technical concerns to refining your survival strategies. Remember, The Forest is about adaptation and ingenuity. Use these tips as a starting point, not a strict guide. Experiment, improvise, and let your instincts guide you through the wilds. With grit and resourcefulness, thrive in The Forest's cannibal-infested landscape.

Chapter 9

Community Resources

Embarking into The Forest's perilous wilderness can be daunting, but fear not – you're not alone in this adventure. Joining forces with a vibrant and supportive community can make your journey not only survivable but genuinely enjoyable. Here's your compass to explore the plethora of resources at your disposal:

Links to Relevant Forums and Communities

- **The Forest Official Forums:**

Your go-to hub endorsed by the developers, housing official announcements, bug reports, deep discussions, and even Q&A sessions. A treasure trove for answers and connecting with fellow survivors.

- **r/TheForest on Reddit:**

A bustling community sharing tips, base designs, eerie encounters, and problem-solving discussions. Unearth specific solutions, hidden secrets, and engage in lively conversations.

- **Discord Servers:**

Dive into various servers catering to your playstyle, be it casual gaming, speedrunning, building, or lore exploration. Connect with kindred spirits among fellow survivors.

Recommended Videos and Livestreams

- **YouTube Guides:**

For those who learn visually, channels like Yamn, TheRelaxingEnd, and BdoubleO offer guides, walkthroughs, and entertaining Let's Plays. Specialized channels focus on combat, building, or uncovering hidden areas.

- **Twitch Streams:**

Watch skilled players tackle The Forest live. CohhCarnage, AdmiralBahroo, and Zizaran provide gameplay, commentary, and viewer interaction, offering a dynamic learning experience.

- **Creative Community Content:**

Explore fan-made content on YouTube, from music videos to cinematic trailers and animated shorts set in The Forest. Witness breathtaking base designs, resource maps, and lore analyses on dedicated websites.

In-Person Experiences:

- **Conventions and Events:**

Immerse yourself in The Forest community at gaming conventions. Share stories, meet players, and grab exclusive merchandise to enhance your real-world connection.

- **Fan Art and Cosplay:**

Delve into the game's unique atmosphere through fan art on DeviantArt and Reddit. Marvel at illustrations, comics, and 3D models, and witness cosplayers bringing The Forest's characters to life.

Golden Rules:

- **Engage and Contribute:**

Don't just consume – share your experiences, tips, and discoveries. Contribute to the positive atmosphere that defines The Forest community.

- **Respect and Courtesy:**

Treat everyone with respect, acknowledging diverse opinions and playstyles. Remember, we're all survivors facing the same challenges.

- **Have Fun!**

While The Forest is challenging, don't forget the joy of exploration and overcoming obstacles.

Cherish the shared experience and camaraderie that brought you into the game.

By embracing the wealth of resources and the communal spirit of The Forest, you'll not only endure the island's horrors but forge enduring friendships and unforgettable memories. So, with axe in hand, head held high, and the community at your side, boldly venture forth and conquer The Forest!

Chapter 10

Unveiling The Forest's Hidden Mysteries

Explore beyond survival in The Forest, where a realm of mysteries awaits the inquisitive adventurer. This section delves into the concealed depths of the island, exposing expert strategies and elusive treasures that can either tip the scales in your favor or captivate your curiosity.

Expert Tactics for Discovering Concealed Items

- Harmony with the Wind:

Uncover secrets by attuning to unique tones produced by specific wind chimes. Crafting bone chimes that match these tones reveals concealed doors and covert passages.

- Embrace the Shadows:

Navigate caves and bunkers effectively during the night using a flare gun. Ignite strategically placed oil barrels to illuminate hidden pathways and activate mechanisms.

- Ghostly Whispers:

Listen closely to spectral voices in certain caves for cryptic clues leading to hidden stashes or unique crafting materials.

- Unusual Alliances:

Befriend a passive albino cannibal for insights into undiscovered locations and rare crafting materials.

- Guidance from the Departed:

Craft skull lamps from enemies' skulls to uncover hidden levers or pressure plates. Use them like divining rods to reveal secret caches and activate concealed mechanisms.

- Chasing Sunbeams:

Look for sunbeams penetrating cave walls to discover hidden passages or secret chambers behind waterfalls.

- Architect's Mindset:

Experiment by placing logs and rocks in seemingly insignificant locations to trigger hidden events or unlock secret doors.

- Dare the Glitch:

Clever players have discovered glitches allowing access to unreachable areas or clipping through walls. Caution: exploits may have unintended consequences and corrupt save files.

Hidden Commands and Quick Shortcuts

- **Invincibility:** Activate god mode with "developermode activategod," but be wary of diminishing the challenge and sense of achievement.

- **Skyward Soar:** Utilize "developermode enableflight" to explore the island from the skies.

- **Dimensional Passage:** Use "noclip" cautiously to pass through obstacles, recognizing its potential to break immersion.

- **Item Manifestation:** Spawn any item with "spawn [item name]" for testing builds or casual experimentation.

- **Weather Control:** Manage elements with "developermode changeweather sun," "developermode changeweather rain," or "developermode changeweather fog."

- **Story Jump:** Bypass specific story elements with "developermode jumptostorymarker [marker name]," acknowledging potential disruptions to game progression.

- **Swift Travel:** Teleport to discovered locations with "goto [location name]" for efficient exploration.

- **Time Manipulation:** Instantly change time with "day" or "night" commands for convenience.

- **Item Direct Delivery:** Spawn any item by entering its ID with "give item_id" for testing or early acquisition.

- **Hourly Adjustment:** Change the time of day instantly with "time [hour]" for timely events like the plane crash cutscene.

- **Debug Insights:** Unlock "debug_mode" for advanced tools like collision boxes, object IDs, and AI pathfinding visualization.

Remember, using cheat commands can diminish the thrill of exploration. Treat them as tools for experimentation, not shortcuts to victory.

Hidden Artifact Chronicles

- **The Skull Lantern:** Discover a hidden chamber marked by a skull in the Sinkhole Caves, offering it to the cannibal effigy for the perpetual Skull Lantern.

- **The Golden Armor:** Collect and place eight golden masks on mannequins beneath the plane crash site to unlock the formidable Golden Armor.

- **The Tennis Racket:** Solve a platform puzzle activated by a secret lever behind the net in the eastern coast tennis court to obtain the surprisingly powerful Tennis Racket.

- **The Secret Ending:** Uncover an alternate ending by completing challenging tasks and deciphering cryptic clues, unraveling more about the island's history and Timmy's fate.

While commands reveal the game's inner workings, genuine satisfaction lies in unraveling mysteries independently. Keep an eye out for anomalies, cryptic symbols, and unusual sounds. Experiment with tools and resources, and embrace the unknown. The Forest rewards the curious and dedicated, unveiling profound secrets to those venturing off the beaten path.

This chapter is a starting point. Delve deeper, discover easter eggs, hidden lore, and developer messages. Share your findings, discuss theories, and contribute to The Forest's ever-growing secrets.

Remember, the game's greatest treasures aren't always tangible. The thrill of the hunt, the joy of overcoming challenges, and the satisfaction of uncovering hidden truths are rewards surpassing any secret item or cheat code. Arm yourself with knowledge, skepticism, and curiosity for an adventure into The Forest's true secrets.

Chapter 11

Conclusion

Final Thoughts and Encouragement

As the dying embers of your final campfire fade along the volcanic shore, casting lingering shadows upon the rugged silhouette of the island, a poignant sense of closure envelops you. The Forest, once a turbulent dance of primal fear and unyielding strife, has unveiled its secrets, both enchanting and grotesque. You stand, bearing scars but unwavering, a testament to the indomitable human spirit confronting unfathomable perils.

Traversing this cannibal-infested wilderness has become an odyssey of self-discovery. Sharpened instincts, a crafted destiny, and battles with inner and outer demons define your journey. Coexisting with the primal rhythms of the forest, you've learned to respect its power while etching your path through the lush labyrinth.

The memory of Timmy, your son, flickers in your heart. His absence resonates in rustling leaves and haunting mutant cries. Yet, it's a wellspring of strength, a reminder of love propelling you, and hope fueling defiance against the encroaching darkness.

Grief, akin to the forest, forms a complex ecosystem, harboring shadows of despair and fertile grounds for resilience. Loss's weight shapes your resolve, emphasizing life's preciousness and the value inherent in each sunrise.

Emerging from the verdant embrace of The Forest, you step into a metamorphosed world. No longer the lost and bewildered soul from the crash, you're a survivor, a warrior, a testament to enduring human will. Scars of hardship meld with wisdom gained in the crucible of adversity.

The rustle of leaves and distant bird calls no longer send shivers without invoking a spark of triumph. You stared into the abyss and blinked. Wrestling primal forces, you emerged victorious.

Now, at the brink of a new chapter, the island, once a prison, transforms into a stepping stone. The world awaits, its possibilities as vast and untamed as the conquered wilderness. Share experiences, guide others, or silently carry learned lessons, a warrior forever marked by The Forest's crucible.

Regardless of your path, the lessons from the green embrace transcend this island. Universal truths applicable to any life challenge: embrace the unknown, confront fears, and never cease learning, crafting, and adapting. Seize the opportunity to explore, construct, and triumph over the world that awaits you.

As you venture forth, carrying echoes of the forest within, remember Timmy. Let his memory be a beacon, a reminder that even in the darkest nights, the sun rises.

Acknowledgments and Credits

This guide owes its existence to countless individuals investing heart and soul into The Forest. To Endnight Games' talented developers, thank you for crafting this unforgettable world, a blend of terror and beauty captivating millions. To the player community, your shared knowledge, strategies, and stories enriched the experience. And to you, dear reader, thank you for this journey. May the lessons guide you through life's metaphorical and literal dark forests.

The true legacy of The Forest lies not only in landscapes and gameplay but in the enduring spirit of players. As this guide concludes, keep the fire burning, share stories, and inspire others with your courage and resilience.

And now, step out of the shadows, survivor. The world awaits.